So...

You want to be a

Journalist?

So...
You want to be a
Journalist?

Dean Short

KOGAN
PAGE

YOURS TO HAVE AND TO HOLD

BUT NOT TO COPY

First published in 1998

Kogan Page Limited
120 Pentonville Road
London N1 9JN

British Library Cataloguing in Publication Data

A CIP record for this book is available from the British Library.

ISBN 0 7494 2757 4

Typeset by JS Typesetting, Wellingborough, Northants.
Printed in England by Clays Ltd, St Ives plc.

Contents

1

Stop press – Are you out of your mind?

So you want to be a journalist? Stop and think. Why do you want to enter this area of work? As a species, journalists are regarded by the public as the lowest of the low – even less deserving of trust than politicians. Journalists themselves accept they don't have the most honourable of professions. No matter how much journalists are relied upon to keep them informed and up to date, the public still loathe the people who produce the headlines. As one new recruit to journalism remarked to me, 'Some people think reporters are there to be yelled at'.

For newcomers to the industry, the first few years of work can be hard to survive. Some editorial offices will be encouraging and no doubt get hard work out of you, but they may not be too keen on paying a decent wage – or even any wage at all. And, at worst, some 'traineeships' run by publishers, are simply an excuse for cheap labour and give you few skills other than operating the photocopier and making tea. The path to recognition and a decent pay packet is long and arduous. There are many pitfalls along the way and all manner of boring, loathsome jobs to do. Perhaps the most important aspect of working in those first years is the process of 'hardening up' whereby you will become immune to the criticism hurled at you by the public and other parts of the press, and will grow increasingly ruthless in nailing down a good story.

For every top investigative journalist there are hundreds of wannabes ploughing out copy on the most mundane subjects. Trainees and recruits have dreams of reviewing the latest news on the artistic and fashion scene – making and breaking talent. Ten or 15 years down the road those dreams may still only be dreams. It takes determination, persistence, luck and a fair amount of flattering your superiors to climb to the top of the profession.

Make no mistake, there is no job like journalism. Where else can you follow world events, talk to interesting and famous people, and get paid to write about what you think? A music reviewer receives hundreds of free CDs and invitations to concerts every week in the hope he will write about them in his next column. Even if your work is not directly related to a product area there are other perks. Press conferences and launches are frequently accompanied by refreshments and 'incentives'. Some media events may be attempts to 'buy coverage' by publicity departments and companies, but journalists can still accept invitations to such events without letting it bias what they write.

Explore the world

Journalism can be the antithesis of a boring office job. As a reporter you will be out and about, travelling around your local patch and searching out stories. You could be a regional reporter for a national paper or a specific section correspondent. There will be opportunities to visit interesting places and meet fascinating people to gather material for your story. But there will also be boring visits to be made – you can spend days sitting in council sessions or at the local courts, just in case something interesting occurs. After three or four hours you can conclude nothing exciting will happen so off you go and cover another local resident's hundredth birthday party.

As a fully trained and competent journalist, you are not limited to one single medium. Indeed, in today's information-rich society, it is a positive disadvantage to be literate only within one news outlet. The basic skills of collecting, analysing and presenting information are the same whether you work in print, radio, television or across the Internet. All you need to do is gain the presentation skills specific to that medium.

Uncertain hours can be the most exciting and also the most frustrating aspect of working as a journalist. News events do not wait for journalists to arrive before they take place. People connected with major events may decide not to talk to the press or be elusive to contact. Reporters can find themselves dragged out of bed or away from social engagements by an editor keen to get someone working on a breaking news story.

Anti-social hours are also likely in newsrooms providing reports around the clock. News agency staff have always worked shifts, as have staff in broadcast newsrooms in radio and television. Initiatives such as the BBC's recently introduced 24-hour rolling news service and Internet news sites have abolished publishing deadlines, calling instead on journalists to continually update news stories as they break and develop.

Even magazine journalists are likely to find themselves working long and unpredictable hours in the run-up to a publication going to press. Editors, sub-editors, reporters and feature writers can find themselves still plugging away at text well into the night, desperate to finish before the ultimate deadline. Monthly and bi-monthly publications have longer run-up times to publication, but it can still be very stressful to put them together. Such magazines tend to be published three or four weeks before the month they are intended to cover. This means news items and fashion pieces need a great deal of foresight and planning. No amount of preparation can prevent last-minute panic as copy from one journalist is lost or photographic material does not arrive. What makes matters worse is that pulling together all of this material is frequently the responsibility of two or three full-time staff – everything else is produced by freelance journalists away from the office. But freelances beware: if there happens to be a spare page going and extra copy required, a quick phone call could mean a sleepless night for you too.

If you already have a passion for a particular subject you may find it easy to write about the latest developments in the field. For instance, Tony Parsons started out writing for the *New Musical Express* magazine when he was close to the music scene himself. From these beginnings he has established himself as a popular culture critic. He's travelled all over the world, writing features for various magazines. It's no surprise to find that he can't think of a better way of making a living.

Journalism keeps you in touch with the real world. You can't afford to get insular or obsessed with office politics. Your work is not limited by what your employer wants to do, but by what happens in the world. Journalists provide the link between the outside world and the general public – whether it be international current affairs or the latest UK pop sensation.

The romantic writer

Perhaps your reason for wanting to become a journalist is simply because you enjoy writing. You like using words, so whether you end up writing about two valiant pigs escaping from a slaughter-house in Wiltshire or another member of the royal family caught at an embarrassing moment, it doesn't matter. You may have a romantic image of yourself as a diligent writer, searching for the right word for your incisive copy.

Leaf through any paper or magazine on the subject of the media and you'll find advertisements which cash in on this romantic image. Correspondent writing schools claim it's dead easy to make money out of writing and that anyone can learn how to do it in their spare time. Such schools boast great success with many of their students. In fact, the most important lesson these schools can teach you is that there are thousands of publications in the UK ready to pay authors for their work. Being successful is more a matter of finding the publication which is interested in what you have to say than improving your own writing skills.

An equally romantic image is that of the investigative journalist, door-stepping the guilty and revealing unjust practices in public and private life. You may see yourself as the journalist who will not take no for an answer, will bash away at copy late into the night and then dash into the editorial office first thing in the morning shouting for the editor to hold the front page.

Press invasion and politics

This side of journalism has a puzzling, contradictory nature to it. The public hate journalists for encroaching on private grief, for sensationalizing stories and for intruding into the private lives of the rich and famous. But at the same time it is precisely this kind of journalism which guarantees the biggest audience for the news.

The death of Diana, Princess of Wales, in August 1997 revealed this dichotomy particularly well. Diana was the most photographed person in the world. Not a week went by when she did not appear in the newspapers, on television or radio. Shunning attention on the one hand yet courting publicity on the other as she did, exclusive photographs of her could command extremely high fees from newspaper and magazine editors.

Some believe she was literally pursued to death by 'paparazzi' photographers still trying to get that exclusive photo. The tabloid papers which had paid large sums for such material were accused of having contributed towards her death, but these publications claimed they were merely satisfying the demands of the general public. At least one paper performed a complete about turn on their coverage of Diana, pandering entirely to the demands of their readership. Having previously been critical of her as an uncaring mother, the paper switched sides seamlessly to pay her glowing tributes as an icon of our times.

The issue is a quagmire. We expect a free press to deliver reports on the issues of the day, and indeed the press is praised when it discovers and highlights examples of wrong doing. But the lines are blurred between what constitutes reporting in the public interest, reporting on the grounds of public demand and reporting which takes a step too far into the private lives of others.

Very often the view one takes of press activities simply reflects a political bias. No national newspaper is free of party political bias (although *The Independent* has made a fairly good job of it) and, indeed, this is important in the reporting of the news: readers want to read something which supports their view of the world (which could be one reason why *The Independent* is not the most popular paper on the news stands). Broadcast news – on TV and radio – is expected to have even more integrity. Certainly, political bias on the BBC – supported by the licence payers themselves – can never be tolerated.

Journalists have a hard time with politicians. During the election in May 1997, many people felt the news was being manipulated by 'spin doctors' – people employed specifically to get advantageous news coverage for their political party. At the same time, politicians criticized news programmes for dictating areas of debate and trying to create discord where there was agreement. There is now something of a tradition of leaked memos and faxes from government departments to the press. In some instances these appear to have been genuine enough – revealing the true intent of a minister and his policy or providing an insight into the back-room machinations of government. But there are also apparent instances of intentionally leaked information. At one point it seemed the government was 'accidentally' releasing details of its latest ideas for legislation to the press in order to gauge public reaction to the ideas and then introduce something slightly less radical.

These issues have been played over so many times now, that the news itself is frequently discussed in the news. We are living in a media-wise age where everybody understands public relations. The journalists' customers – the readers, listeners and viewers – are aware of how facts can be manipulated and quotes interpreted. The news can now include reports of a politician complaining about the way the news is reported. In the case of the death of Princess Diana, one newspaper distanced itself from the massive coverage of her life, death and all the repercussions surrounding the events by writing about the massive coverage of her life, death and all the repercussions . . .

As newspapers have fought each other for readership, a circulation war has developed, claiming many casualties in the past few years.

News in print and on the television has taken no prisoners to secure the support of greater percentages of the population and it could be said that in this war, the first casualty has been the truth. Media commentators and journalists alike bemoan the state of journalism in the UK and internationally, claiming that the whole industry is now concerned with turning matters of great importance into pure light entertainment.

You're responsible

So what does this mean for you as you sit down in front of your keyboard for the first day's work? One word: pressure. You are at the front line of these issues. You are the person who will receive all the information relating to a subject; the facts, the attractive public relations blurbs, the cautious press releases and words spoken in an unguarded moment. It is up to you to filter this information, decide what is relevant, what is irrelevant, what is biased and what is true. You decide what the story is.

At the same time, whatever you write, it must be interesting enough to attract the reader or catch the attention of viewers or listeners. A good by-line won't be adequate; you must provide facts, figures, quotes – real proof to back up your story. You must also be able to present that story in a way which guarantees your readers do not stray until the story is finished.

Remember, everything you report will have an impact on someone somewhere. You may have the opportunity to bring a startling new story to the homes of millions – the impact of a series of reports on the famine in Africa in the mid 1980s changed many people's lives. It inspired a national charity campaign, a global pop concert and continued charity events to this day. Your piece of writing might spell fame and fortune for one person, complete disaster for someone else. It may sell thousands of newspapers, attract millions of viewers or listeners. It may propel you to the higher echelons of journalism. But if it is wrong – if there are inaccuracies or you have skewed the facts to suit your own story – you may never work again. There have been many celebrated cases of legal action taken against the media by disgruntled people who find themselves the subject of public speculation. Unless a journalist can substantiate his story, a whole publication may be put out of business through a lost libel case.

As a reporter you have a responsibility to your audience. How you handle that responsibility is up to you. Even if you do not have editorial control you will determine the impact of the story – the points which everyone will remember. Journalism is a question of ethics: what are your priorities in writing? Accuracy, precision and information? Or entertainment and titillation? An exposition of hypocrisy, or scandalmongering around those in the public eye? For some people the idea of a journalist with ethics is a contradiction in terms – and to succeed in writing for some publications it is true you must stop at nothing to get the story you want.

The belief that high standards of journalism automatically result in a successful journalist is sadly a little wide of the mark. No magazine or newspaper is fully supported by the cover price paid by its readers. The key to the business is attracting high levels of advertising. In some cases – particularly trade and small circulation consumer magazines – the equation between advertising revenue and editorial copy is such that journalists are really only employed to fill the space between the advertisements. A publication is successful because of the standard of journalism carried within its pages – but this is because advertisers perceive the publication to be read by the people to whom they wish to sell. They will therefore take out more advertising according to the amount and type of readership, and thus boost the revenue of the publication.

Techno prisoners

In past years journalism was a strongly unionized occupation. However, new technology introduced at the end of the 1980s changed the way newspapers were produced. Desk-top publishing packages mean today's journalists and editors can place copy directly on to a computer screen which will then create the final page of print.

As a result of this, the industry has undergone a 'churn' in employment: traditional journalists lost their jobs, but they were replaced by newcomers to the industry who were technology literate. The result of this is that the same number of journalists are employed today, but they are now from a higher socio-economic group than, say, five years ago. Journalism has moved from being regarded as a trade to being a profession. Today's journalist is likely to be white, male and university educated. Ethnic minorities are poorly represented in the industry and women still have a hard time gaining promotion and even avoiding harassment in the workplace.

While the situation may be improving, the large established market for women's lifestyle and fashion magazines has not resulted in better status for women. National magazines and daily newspapers can boast of only a few women at editorial levels. Journalists may have moved away from being the stereo-typical hack, but the industry maintains a hard-living, stressed-out, macho image. Journalists are expected to be committed to their publication and that means hard work, late nights and taking risks.

The demise of the chain-smoking, hard-lunchtime-drinking journalist may be the result of the 'employment churn' but equally it may simply illustrate the way in which editorial offices have changed. Publishers and broadcasters have dispensed with employing full-time reporters, in favour of using freelance contrib-utors. Magazines and local newspapers are now run with a skeleton staff – reporters on the latter even writing advertorial copy as well as real newspaper reports. This has increased the pressure on office-based staff to co-ordinate news reports, leaving no time for even a swift drink at lunchtime. One local reporter noted that even when a great story had been splashed across the front page there was little opportunity to go down the pub and celebrate.

But at the end of the day, the hard work is worth it. There's nothing like the buzz you get when your first article is published and your name is in print. There's a great feeling of recognition – that you have arrived and people will take notice of you. As your career progresses you may find you are recognized by readers and other commentators in your field. You may be considered an important person to know because of the influence you have and your overview of the world you are writing about. Perhaps the highlight of a newspaper journalist's career is when you are offered your own column in which you can express your own views on whatever you feel moved to comment on.

At the same time, journalism is extremely fickle and fashion conscious. What makes a good subject, a good feature, even a good magazine or news programme today may not continue to deliver the goods two or three years down the line. You must always be flexible in what you write about and how you write about it. To survive you need to tap into the 'Zeitgeist' – the spirit of the age – and try to predict what people need to know about in the future.

2

The right to write (Qualifications and what they don't lead to)

Training for journalism is at the moment in a bit of a mess. It's not that there are no well-structured, coherent, well-run courses offering journalistic skills for all media requirements, it is that there is a profusion of such courses – academic, vocational, general and specific – and no recognized structure in which such courses can be measured. Enthusiastic would-be journalists are currently faced with all these courses and no indication of how any qualifications they may achieve are valued in the workplace.

It used to be the case that a young journalist would enter the profession, do at least three years on a local paper in order to earn their stripes, gain a certificate from the National Council for the Training of Journalists (NCTJ) and then move on to their first real job. Certification from the NCTJ or BJTC (Broadcast Journalism Training Council) is still a popular way into the industry for many journalists and the qualification can be gained from many journalism college 'pre-entry' courses up and down the UK. However, you could also go to college or university and take a media course, gain a BA or even an MA in journalism. Alternatively you could take an HND or BTEC in the subject; gain a postgraduate certificate or diploma, or obtain recognition from an independent training company. Another option is to join your first employer with no vocational qualifications at all but build them up through training on the job or the company's own in-house training scheme.

In the future another training option will join these choices: the Modern Apprenticeship will offer work-based training towards National Vocational Qualifications (NVQ) – a useful addition to the paths above since they are generally more suited to those who prefer academic tuition. Modern Apprenticeships are established and administered by the National Training Organization for each industry sector. This presents a problem for the journalism sector because, at the moment, there are four training organizations: The Newspaper Society (newspapers); Skillset (broadcasting); the Periodicals Training Council (periodicals and magazines); and Book House (book publishing). None of these particularly want to step down from their position of influence and some refuse to discuss the subject with other organizations. In addition, the Guild of Editors has recently proposed a new qualification for editors at diploma level which falls outside all other frames of reference for training entirely.

Each of these options will give you (in varying amounts) practical skills including basic word-processing, politics (structure of local and national government), the theory and history of journalism and the study of journalistic law. Training establishments may provide work placements or have their own newsrooms set up so students get some real, practical experience.

To train or not to train?

What kind of training do you need? It depends on the kind of journalism you want to do. You may find you need none at all: there are many full-time professional journalists who have received no training whatsoever. They may have started out simply as researchers for publishers or broadcasters and gradually built up the necessary skills. I fall into the 'untrained' category. I taught myself the discipline of writing to a set number of words and interviewing people, effectively providing myself with on-the-job training.

On the other hand one journalist I know did take a radio broadcast journalism course. The course taught students how to cut and edit sound tape (a skill she already had thanks to previous work experience) and all students had to pass a journalism law exam. In a way this is the most important aspect of official training. When you're working under pressure you have to know instantly what you can or can't say in your news report. You must realize the full implications of what you are about to publish. In this respect, getting an NCTJ or BJTC certificate means a news editor knows you are already prepared for work in a newsroom. This radio journalist described how her training had enabled her to 'leap frog' into the position of reporter or news editor, able to take on the responsibilities at this level without having had to gain skills and knowledge through years of on-the-job experience.

The training centre she attended had its own operating newsroom which students had to keep running 12 hours a day, working early and late shifts. The newsroom had its own link to the news agencies, and students took it in turns to work as reporters, sports, arts and programme editors. The newsroom had to operate as reports came in throughout the day and was at first extremely frightening to work in. Principally it was the pressure of getting a story which the students found alarming. Sometimes they would be set projects to go and find stories in random locations or on specific subjects. They would have to do the research, find the story and report back within their deadline. While starting out may have been terrifying, training this way meant she was able to make her mistakes in a safe environment. When she left the training centre she was fully prepared for the day-to-day work of a professional newsroom.

On the other hand, a newspaper journalist explained that during her training she took two days a week work experience at a local newspaper. She believes real journalistic skills can only be gained on the job. In her case, college had taught her nothing of the pressure of working to deadlines or even of how to phone up and interview people for an article.

One sub-editor I spoke to took an English degree at university and went into a major magazine publishing house. During her first year she was given a wide range of courses to train her up for the job. Most were provided in-house, covering subbing skills, news writing, feature writing and so on. Training in Quark, the computer programme used to lay out the magazine pages, was sourced outside the company and was, according to the trainee, the most useful training she received for her job. In-house training on creating text – how to write news stories, features and interviews – is very common since it gives the publisher a chance to make sure journalists understand the style and subject matter required for each publication.

A degree in economics, medicine or any other specific area is just as likely to get you into journalism as a vocational course. One journalist I know created quite a reputation for himself in writing for a magazine which covered the use of and changes in metal technology. He came to the publication having spent a couple of years at British Steel following an economics degree. It was clear he had the writing skills required by the publisher, but more importantly he had the contacts and knew how to speak to people in the industry and to interpret what they had to say. He did not particularly feel attached to the subject, but was more than happy to be writing on a subject he knew about and to be invited around the world to speak at industry conferences.

Another magazine editor, who came to journalism as a second career, underwent no official training. Instead he was given a 'mentor' from within the organization, someone who would be able to point him in the right direction and smooth over any difficulties he experienced in bringing the publication together.

To some extent, technology has removed the need for specific skills from the industry – after all, who doesn't know how to work a word processor these days? Instead, publishers are looking to attract specialist writers who can demonstrate complete understanding of their subject.

Expert witnesses

Specialist magazines employ expert writers with well-developed analytical abilities as well as research skills and useful contacts. You may not have gained your expertise through a degree or further education: the market in magazines and periodicals now covers every subject you can name, from toy train sets through to construction work, and there are a whole host of magazines connected to clubs and companies and interest groups the public never get to see. You might find that knowledge you have gained through the pursuit of a hobby puts you in the ideal situation to write about it professionally. Accuracy and accessibility are at a premium here: there's no point in writing up an in-depth report in such a way that no one understands what you're on about.

Skills in information technology (IT) can put you at an advantage in the printed media. If you are able to work with QuarkXpress, you will be able to lay out pages of newspaper. As such you will find it easier to move up to a post like section editor where these skills are required. Alternatively, you may be able to move into sub-editing and production. If you are familiar with the software for writing pages on the World Wide Web you may be particularly useful to publishers who now regard this area as the next place for expansion.

It is possible, however, to start work in journalism without any industry-specific skills. Whether in-house or as a freelance writer, if you can produce good copy you are likely to be able to find work in some capacity. From that point onwards it will become clear which skills you need – be they computer related, touch-typing or shorthand. These skills can be gained through in-house or external training courses. There are thousands of courses in shorthand and many colleges will give you Quark training.

As a feature and book writer I do not have shorthand and cannot touch-type. Both of these skills would help me in my day-to-day work, but not having them does not prevent me from working effectively. If I wanted to work in a newsroom or as a full-time reporter I would need these skills immediately. A local news reporter explained that shorthand was probably the most useful skill she had learned at college simply because she does not have time to use a dictaphone. The pace of feature writing is slower than news gathering and usually the copy benefits from a longer consideration of the material.

The best advice is to decide where you want to work and then find out the training you require – otherwise you could spend years following a course which does not put you where you want to be. The other thing to consider is the best way in which you learn. Don't keep applying for academic courses if you are not academically gifted. There are many different ways of working in the industry and many different ways to get there. Once you're in your first position you will immediately start to learn. Even if you're only making the tea you'll see how the publication puts together stories, how journalists liaise with contacts and assemble the material for broadcast or publication. You'll gain workplace skills – working with other people towards a common result – which no amount of training will give you.

How to write proper

The most maddening thing about journalists and careers teachers who talk about what skills are needed for the job is that they will always tell you to be a journalist you must be able to write good English. A swift glance at the tabloid newspapers and many style magazines will show you this is a load of rubbish.

Yes, journalists do need to be able to write good English, but more important than grammatical correctness is the ability to write something which will be read by your publication's readership. These two writing styles are not necessarily the same thing. It's well known that text in *The Sun* newspaper is pitched roughly at the reading age of a three year old. In the majority of tabloids – and even more upmarket publications – headlines can bear little or no resemblance to proper use of the English language at all. Good writers can make a story flow, entertain and inform their readers at the same time – but the way this is done for readers of *The Stage* and *Television Today* will be completely different than for readers of *Just 17* magazine or any of the national dailies. It's not about content, it's about style.

For some journalists, grammatical correctness is more important than for others. Sub-editors are sometimes employed on newspapers and magazines to ensure articles submitted fit the space on the page and adhere to the use of English suitable for that publication. It's meticulous work, sifting through copy provided by journalists for inaccuracies. Sub-editors need an awareness of current affairs and legal matters to avoid possibly libellous material. Writing in grammatical English may be one thing, but it's a different matter if your report is for broadcast. Choosing the right words for the right occasion and not tripping over word order can be extremely difficult.

My introduction to the idea of being a journalist came at a careers fair at school. The journalist taking the session began by saying: 'If you want to be a journalist you must always be asking questions. Never take no for an answer.' At the end of his presentation no one had any questions for him at all – which should have ruled every one of us out of the industry. The idea of forever enquiring into other people's business did not appeal to me at the time. I liked the idea of writing and playing around with words, but when it came to hard-hitting research I'd really rather not. In my particular area the research I do is rarely controversial or revelatory and most people are happy to chat about the things I need to discuss. So, again, it is possible to take quite a relaxed approach to journalism enquiries.

What is it?

The one personality trait shared by all journalists is straightforward curiosity. From the door-stepping tabloid hack to the business writer phoning a contact in the city, they all want to know how things work, why things happen and who made them happen like that in the first place. Learning how to ask the right question is a matter of experience. When I started, my interviews had a tendency to last around 30 minutes each and ultimately yield two or three lines of quotable text. It is true some of that interview serves as background information for the report, but as you get more into your subject you can be more searching and precise with the questions you ask.

Broadcast journalists take interviewing skills a step further. There's little point in recording material from an interviewee who says nothing remotely interesting or usable. You need to ensure sound levels are high enough, that the background noise does not interfere and finally that the questions you ask elicit good responses. One radio journalist explained to me that very often the only way to get material is to let the interviewee answer in their own way the first time and then ask them to repeat the point in a more concise manner.

In television, the process is further complicated by the need to get 'cutaway' shots of the interviewer asking the interviewee questions. Interviews are usually shot with only one camera, but just looking at the interviewee all the time is visually boring. Therefore the interview is shot first, and then reverse views of the interviewer will be taken and edited into the report for broadcast. This means the reporter has to remember precisely the wording of the questions they ask – no mean feat if an interview goes off in an unexpected direction.

Multiskilling is proliferating within the industry. Just as radio reporters are expected to gather interview material and cut together their own news items – with or without the producer's guidance – television journalists are now having to acquire the same kind of skills.

A single reporter will be sent out with a camera to cover a particular story. The reporter will have to interview those connected with the story, film pictures and sound on site, and then take this back and edit it in order to tell the story to the viewers. Reporters might have to record voice-overs to add clarity to the report and prepare a brief for the newscaster so the item can be introduced properly and slotted into the running order of the programme.

Working in this way may mean you need technical skills alongside specific journalism skills. Journalism is an uncertain industry. You never know whether your work will continue to be in demand from editors or whether the entire publication will be bought up, go bust or revamped, leaving you without work. One way to protect yourself from this is to ensure you have the skills to cope with journalism in all media and across many different subjects. It may not be possible for you to get these skills without some financial investment. However you can – and should – start working on your journalism skills immediately.

The one skill you will need from day one until the last day you work in the industry is one you can prove regardless of academic or vocational training, and one which you can even have without being published. That is the ability to write. If you gain general journalism skills you can report on any subject – be it the local Darby and Joan Club outing or a gig by the latest pop group. The skills of research, interpretation and presentation will always stand you in good stead. So, if you're a student, write for a student magazine; if there isn't one, set one up. Write to your local paper and try out articles on them, or just write material for the sake of putting together an article so you know what it feels like and how it should be structured. Only by doing it will you discover if it's something you can and would like to dedicate the rest of your life to.

3

How hot is your metal?
(Finding the right doors
to knock on)

The news-gathering industry conforms to very few rules of promotion and even pays scant regard to experience. You may be able to plan your ascendancy through a publishing house or with a newspaper, from report writing to feature writing to editorship, but it is more likely that your lucky break will come out of the blue. Gaining status as a reporter may come through tireless hard work – Kate Adie (BBC TV) has built a strong reputation for herself through years of reporting from war zones around the world. Alternatively, an increase in your pay packet may simply be the result of being able to nail down the story or interview everybody else was after. One well-known journalist got her big break when she chased after a taxi and got herself in the back of the vehicle with a celebrity who proceeded to give her the story of their acrimonious divorce.

Not all journalists are looking for promotion in a newsroom, broadcast or newsprint publication. Climbing the ladder in such places may mean rising from reporter to commissioning editor – or in the case of radio and television – to the position of producer. As such you will no longer be out reporting yourself. You will spend your time glued to the phone, lining up stories and interviews for other reporters to go out and get. Some journalists do not like being left in the office while the young reporters go out and have all the fun.

In the same way it is often thought that local papers are merely the proving ground for new hacks and that reporters here will ultimately graduate to the national newspapers. In truth, local reporting can be equally satisfying as you get to know your area intimately and can sniff out local corruption and scandals from the comfort of your own editorial office.

Success is not simply a matter of being a competent journalist. Placing and selling your story is as important – if not more important – as the quality of the material itself. So how can you succeed in gaining the recognition your incisive writing deserves? Let's start by looking at the day-to-day slog of being a journalist and work up from there.

How to do it

Finding, researching, developing and writing a piece of journalism can be extremely stimulating. It can satisfy your own curiosity about the subject you are writing on and enable you to get to grips with up-to-the-minute information on a particular subject. The process can also be the most frustrating, boring, tiring and terrifying things you can do with your day.

First: find your story. If you are a full-time employee of a newspaper, local or national, it is unlikely that you will be able to dictate what you write about. In all newsrooms everyone is encouraged to put forward ideas for stories and articles, but at the end of the day it is the editor who decides what actually makes it through to the final publication. Radio and television newsrooms and agencies are much the same: there will be many reporters whose job it is to keep track of events in a particular area – foreign news, local news, sport, arts and so on – and there will be some to and froing of ideas between writers and reporters and editors. At the end of the day, however, it is up to the editor to decide which subjects will be followed up and which left to fester.

The editor – whether the section editor of a national paper, principal editor of a local newspaper, the managing editor of a magazine, or the editor of a broadcast news programme – will then allot stories to reporters. If you are lucky the story will come with a straightforward brief – either written down or verbally explained. Alternatively, the story may be well established already, requiring you simply to update a previous report rather than beginning with a completely blank page.

Sometimes the brief you receive is left wide open: 'Do an article of 1500 words about pop music in the Himalayas', for example. This can be a little daunting as you're going to have to start research from scratch. You'll need to root around in phone directories and through a whole load of lifestyle magazines to trace anyone who might have some opinion on the subject. There again, being given free rein can be extremely exciting, allowing you to take the subject in any direction you please. You set the agenda, decide what the angle is and make the piece your own.

The nature of the brief will depend on the type of media you are reporting for and the nature of the story itself. News stories speak for themselves – find out what's happening, who's involved, what's going to happen next and what it all means. The brief for a feature article in a trade publication may tell you precisely what the story is, the angle the publication wants you to take on it, and provide names and numbers of people to talk to.

In radio, the programme's producer will phone round contacts and develop a story before passing it over to a reporter. They will already have decided what will be said by whom, they may even have an idea of the anecdotes each interviewee should tell and thus brief the reporter on what information and sound effects they should gather. Television reports are also generated between the producer and reporter, but on location it will be the reporter who decides what the story is and how the camera crew should capture the required images and sounds.

Whatever information the brief gives you, it will always include two vital pieces of data: the length of the piece and the deadline by which it must be completed. At this point you stand poised at the start of a great adventure: what will you find out, who will you meet and speak to today? At this point you also start praying that your skills of time management are sharp and you are fully prepared to spend the next few hours glued to the telephone.

The telephone is the best way to start research. Unless you are covering a current event or a press conference where your subjects will be available for interview, you need to track down the right people who you can talk to on your subject. Turning up in person, unannounced, may not go down too well and can waste valuable time.

The Internet can also prove a useful tool for the journalist in search of a story and contacts. Most organizations now have their own web pages which can include press releases and contact details. There are search facilities which will even tell you which public relations (PR) agency represents which company or organization. In some cases it is possible to find and research a story entirely on the Internet – even conducting interviews through email.

So you pick up the phone, dial a phone number and ask to speak to someone you've never ever spoken to before in your life to ask them questions on a subject they know more about than you do. You could be speaking to anyone: they might be in the public eye already and used to such enquiries. They may be ordinary members of the public and completely freaked out by your phone call. They could be company employees, afraid of telling you too much in case they get into trouble. They might refer you to someone else who refers you to someone else who refers you to someone else. You might end up talking to someone in the press office or a PR organization which represents the people you want to contact.

The PR brick wall

As one journalist remarked to me, there can be few more effective ways of preventing anyone from finding out anything about a company or organization than to set up a PR department to take care of all enquiries. They can be the most infuriating of operations to do business with. You expect these people to know something about their clients, but frequently they are simply another level of bureaucracy for you to wade through: they can't find the photos you require, can't provide the figures you ask for and aren't even sure whether the organization you want to contact would really want to contribute to your article.

Sometimes PR agencies fall over themselves trying to be helpful – sending you all manner of publicity material, facts and figures to ensure you cannot conceive of a single word against their client – hell, they'll even write the piece for publication themselves if you really want. This can equally hamper the journalist's work – I was once repeatedly phoned up and harassed by a PR executive, desperate to get coverage for one of his clients. He still persisted regardless of the fact that I'd already told him his client was not suitable for anything I was writing about.

PR agencies can set up interviews for you – and this is certainly an invaluable service if you are trying to speak to a single person from a massive organization on a specific subject. They may even allow you to speak directly with that person without their representative being on hand to make sure the questions you ask aren't too searching or difficult to answer.

No matter who you end up speaking to you can expect a whole host of hidden complications to arise during the research stage. The person you need to speak to will be out. Permanently. You'll spend all afternoon being kept on hold, passed around an organization's switchboard, passed back and forth between organizations which claim the other one is responsible for the information you require. You'll have an hour-long chat to someone who then reveals they are not the right person to talk to on the subject, or your interviewee will answer all your questions in a very helpful manner and then refuse to be quoted on the subject.

Another great trick of interviewees is to complete the interview, appear to be very happy with what they've said and then demand to see a copy of what you've written before it goes to press. It's sad to find that many people who support a free press feel they can't trust it to represent their own views accurately. Interviewees from the legal profession often want to make sure they are seen to explain legal facts correctly and some employees fear they will get into trouble if their comments reveal too much about their company.

It's still no excuse for mistrusting the press – after all it is the responsibility of journalists to make sure their facts are right. In such situations it's best to refuse – or pointedly add that they will receive a copy when it goes to press.

Harassment (strong and weak)

For some stories you will need to get interview material from people who would rather not discuss the subject – through embarrassment, legal reasons or personal grief. It will require tenacity on your part to coerce people into commenting. This element of reporting is one of the most difficult aspects of journalism. Reporters will try all manner of techniques to get the comment they want – from explaining how they just want to give their subject the chance to state their side of the story, all the way through to aggressive and invasive questioning. I wouldn't be able to harass someone just to get a front-page scandal headline, but there are journalists who see this as part of the job. At the same time unresponsive interviewees can plague even the least controversial of subjects.

In general it's best to make all your phone calls first thing in the morning so everyone has time to call you back and if you have to go out chasing contacts you've got the afternoon in which to do it. There's an amount of cod psychology behind deciding when the best time is to phone certain people. Clearly, first thing in the morning or in the afternoon – just after your subject has had lunch – you are going to have better results than last thing before they leave in the evening.

It may be that you have to leave the office in order to attend a press conference, to do a face-to-face interview or even 'door-step' your interviewee. You may spend your day dashing from location to location trying to catch up with the people at the centre of your story – interview locals at a crime scene, off to the police station for their viewpoint, then off to the courts, then back to the crime scene for further comment from locals. And while you're chasing that quote, time is running out for your copy deadline.

You may need to trawl through mountains of boring paperwork before you can even start work on a story. Having worked so hard tracking down your interviewee you don't want to blow it all by asking a blatantly obvious question or revealing you have absolutely no grasp of the subject whatsoever. Reporters dedicated to particular sections of the news – business, finance, the arts and so on – will spend some of their time simply reading information in order to keep themselves up to date. They may never need that information for a story but they must have a working and broad knowledge of the subject in order to place stories in context. This knowledge also means you can save time in interviews by asking focused questions rather than trying to get general information. When writing your report you will also have a shrewd idea of what your readership already knows, thereby avoiding condescending to them.

As you carve yourself a path through the information thrown at you from all directions you may discover the story you thought would be ground breaking and shocking is in fact a damp squib. You may have to desert the story altogether and find something else to cover. It may be one of your contacts has provided exciting information, but the others are non-starters, requiring you to think laterally and find other lines of enquiry to follow as quickly as possible. Conversely, you may find your dead-end no-hoper of a story about a cat stuck up in a tree suddenly turns into the story of the month. Until you start researching and talking to people you simply don't know what your story is going to be. It's completely unpredictable, which can be exciting, frustrating and very scary.

Will you, won't you

For this reason the overwhelming emotion, felt by journalists in all media, no matter what the story, is one of controlled panic. When you get your first brief and deadline you think, no problem, loads of time to do it in, I know exactly what it's going to look like and who I'm going to talk to. And then you discover it's not going to be that simple. There is a whole mass of information behind the story which you had no idea existed. You can't find the right people to talk to and you don't think you're going to be able to get your head around the whole thing, let alone put it into words someone else will understand.

Even if it's not panic, chasing a story induces butterflies in the stomachs of many established reporters – and as your story gets better, and you dig deeper, the more nerve-racking the experience becomes. If your investigations are bringing to light a truly amazing story you can guarantee there's a reason why no one has been allowed to write this story before.

However, you finally have a handful of golden quotes, and a brilliant tale to tell. You have a limited number of words in which to tell that story and the deadline is getting closer all the time. Sometimes the story flows perfectly: it's obvious what the main points are and you are able to explain everything exactly for your readers. More often you'll find you have no room at all for the nuances, details and important quotes you have gathered. Sometimes you know you have a good story to tell but cannot work out where you should start telling it. Finding angles and structures on which to hang stories is something that comes with time. Sometimes it feels like there are a number of ways you can start writing about a subject – all you need to do is pick the right one to take you into your story. Finally you end up with a clear, concise article of the right length, just what the brief required, but bereft of any humour and any of the quotes you originally thought would be crucial.

But you hit the deadline! You submit your copy – probably electronically through your own PC – and it winds up on the editor's desk or desk-top computer. At that point the editor reads it, and decides it's OK. The editor may decide it's OK and yet still bombard you with a whole stream of follow-up questions relating to the article ranging from the completely obvious – which you thought were explained fully in the text – to questions you didn't even think to ask. Depending on the deadline you may have to go back and find the required information. If your piece is for printed publication you may have to rewrite considerably in order to incorporate the editor's suggestions. If it is for radio or television there may need to be some careful re-editing carried out. If your piece is too weak and simply doesn't measure up to the editor's expectations it will be dropped – quickly followed by you as a reporter if you waste time like that again.

In a newspaper or magazine scenario, the editor will pass your work on to the sub-editor. The sub-editor proofreads the copy and re-edits it to conform with the publication's in-house style, ensuring their readership will understand and read the article. So far as you're concerned, as the original writer, this process means taking out all your favourite bits and slapping the most horrendous headline across the top. Sub-editors must also make sure the piece fits the appropriate space on the page. If not, it will be cut down in an apparently arbitrary fashion. Sub-editors may have questions for you to clarify the piece, but whatever alterations are made it is extremely unlikely that you, the author, will be consulted in this operation.

The key to success

So how can you ensure that you will be given the breaks you need to push your career forward? The first thing is to be full of ideas. The editor may choose who is going to cover which story, but that choice is more likely to fall with the person who had the idea in the first place or the person who clearly knows the subject area.

If you're working on a local newspaper you may be writing six or seven stories every day. You need to be ready to dig around for the stories that matter – and to take the flak which could accompany such stories. One local reporter told me that if a reader complains about a story then they believe they're doing a good job. Keep your ear to the ground and offer ideas which are not suggested by anyone else. Local papers tend to rely on 'diary' events for their main copy – local events, council machinations and so on – so if you can come up with 'off-diary' events the editor will be impressed. The same applies for other areas of printed media. Section editors of magazines will love you if you can produce well thought-out and original ideas the readers want to know about.

Equally impressive are connections in the professional world. If you have the ear of the movers and shakers of industry, are able to secure interviews with celebrities and get managing directors to talk to you – you will be extremely useful to your editor.

Original ideas are like gold dust. While working on one publication you may decide you'd like to move to a more upmarket publication. Pitch ideas to that editor and use your current experience and reporting as proof of your capability.

Evidence of a ruthless streak when researching and interviewing for reports will get you noticed. But equally you need a ruthless streak in pursuing your own career goals. The best way of getting on in the industry is by knocking on doors. The industry is tough and impressed by people who want to get stuck in and prove themselves. You may have to offer a whole stream of freelance articles to a publication before you convince them they can rely on you as a full-time journalist. When your big break does happen you must be ready to take it with both hands.

Freelances and cut price copy

The rise of freelance work in journalism is unrelenting. Many publishing houses find it financially beneficial to buy in the expertise as and when they require it. Using freelance journalists, a publisher can get professional copy when they want it but only pay for that copy, rather than having to employ a full-time reporter.

Technology has supported this way of working. A journalist can report from anywhere in the country or even around the world, writing copy up on a portable lap-top computer and e-mailing or faxing copy back to the editorial office. Similarly, audio and video reports can be channelled into the newsroom through satellite links, offering news services the chance to show their viewers events from around the world as they happen.

Some full-time journalists see freelances as a threat. They consider they are undermining their own employment status, pandering to the publishers and allowing them to cut costs by farming work out rather than taking the responsibility of supporting a full-time work-force. Freelances, they argue should be used only for providing specialist knowledge, or to cover staff shortages. Part of the resentment against freelances is that their use has reduced union influence in many editorial offices and made it difficult for journalists on any single publication to organize and campaign for improvements in working conditions. Contracts are struck with each individual journalist, making bargaining extremely difficult, especially as each writer does not want to do himself out of a job by demanding too much money for his work.

You do not have to be a reporter to be a freelance. There are also freelance editors and sub-editors, picture researchers and copy readers. Freelances do not necessarily work from their own office – some may work shifts at local or national publications and even on location for broadcast news services. However, anyone with a decent PC can tap into the market for freelance writing and that's a constant source of frustration for those making a living out of freelancing. A large supply of articles increases competition in the market and depresses the price charged for each piece of work.

Freelancing without hunger

The majority of professional freelances have had some experience of full-time work in journalism. This has not only given them the experience and skills to do the job, but also a host of useful contacts – publications which will take their copy and publicity contacts who will help provide stories.

Since freelance journalism is such a precarious profession, many writers have back-up activities to supplement their work. Many writers carry out teaching work, usually part time, and in the further or higher education sector. Others may fit freelance work around housework and rely on their partner for the main income. They may carry out a host of related work for other clients: marketing projects, market research reports or even assembling conferences. Copy writing for newsletters and corporate communication material can also provide lucrative work for freelance journalists.

It is extremely difficult to make a comfortable living from freelance writing alone. Part of the problem is that freelance writers are often competing for space in publications alongside contributors who do not expect to be paid. Academic writers need to be seen to publish their research work in some shape or form and are more than happy to gain this recognition without any financial recompense. There are even cases of 'advertorial' articles – pieces which appear to be unbiased journalism, but which are in fact pushing a company's products and services. Never mind not having to pay for copy, the publication will actually receive payment for publishing these pieces.

And then there are those journalists who, strictly speaking, are not journalists. Celebrity columnists – often with no background in journalism whatsoever – are extremely useful for a newspaper which wants to boost its circulation. If papers sell because of the name of the celebrity rather than the standard of news reporting, the freelancer loses out yet again. It should also be noted that celebrity columns are rarely actually written by those celebs. There will be a very helpful editor or sub-editor behind the text.

Freelancing as a business

Being a freelance journalist is not simply about being a good writer. It's about being a good marketing person and a good business person. Whatever area of work, freelances are constantly dealing with uncertainty. No matter how successful you may be, there is always the fear that one day work will simply dry up and that will be the end of your career. If you can't actually market your skills and ideas as a writer, your career will never exist in the first place.

In the previous chapter, I outlined how an editor decides upon the content of his section, magazine or news programme. As a freelance, you've got to come up with ideas for articles which will compete alongside all the other news stories which land on the editor's desk – from in-house staff, PR agencies and other freelances. It must be a pitch which no editor can refuse. Unfortunately, getting an editor even to consider your ideas can be difficult. Faxing a proposal is more direct than posting it, but the fax may be drowned in hundreds of pitches from other journalists. Having made your pitch, you will want to follow it up with a phone call to the editor to discuss your ideas. You may find it is simply impossible to talk to the editor – either because they are far too busy, or because they have an efficient secretary who's been told not to let them be disturbed by pitching freelances.

So where do you start? I started with market research. I spent weeks and months reading magazines and newspapers to get a feel for what the publications were looking for. I studied their content, style and the length of articles they were publishing. Having done this I phoned up the publications I thought I could contribute to and asked what their policy was on using freelances. Some simply did not welcome any dealings with new freelances at all. Some would look at any material I wanted to send, but couldn't promise any payment or acknowledgement that they'd received my work. Others explained that a letter outlining what I'd like to write about should be sent to the appropriate editor. Further questioning also elicited the name of that editor – frequently a different person to that listed in my *Writers' and Artists' Yearbook*.

I would then concoct my pitching letter and send it off to the publication. Where possible, I'd send several copies of the same pitching letter to different publications – all carefully selected – thereby increasing the number of people who would be considering my ideas. Pitching letters should be no more than one A4 page long and, while being fairly businesslike, should reflect the publication you are writing to as well as your own writing style. Most importantly the letter must show what a brilliant idea your article is, and point out that only you and you alone can write it.

As a new freelance I had one small problem – absolutely no track record whatsoever. For this reason I also spent time writing speculative feature articles. Once again, I'd look through the newspapers and come up with an idea for an article, write it and send it off to that publication. This method is extremely time consuming and may provide no financial remuneration. However, in my case, I succeeded in selling two or three pieces to a national newspaper. With these articles under my belt not only could I include my 'experience' in future pitching letters, but I also had a couple of national newspaper editors who knew who I was and that I could write. Pitching article ideas to these editors was then much easier and, as it turned out, far more lucrative.

You must understand that making any money out of writing articles requires the ability to constantly generate new ideas. There is no way that every idea you have will result in a sale. You're competing with many other journalists, even with in-house teams who are paid salaries to keep ahead of the game and decide which subjects should be covered in the next publication. You will have the same ideas as these people. You will have worse ideas than these people. You will also have much better ideas than these people, but still not be published because your pitch turned up at completely the wrong time in their publishing calendar, or because they simply do not realize what a great story it is you are offering.

I stressed the importance of pitching an article in such a way that it is clear only you can write the piece. The basic reason for this is that you can't copyright an idea. In the mêlée of allocating articles to journalists, it is more than possible that an idea put forward by a freelance could go to an in-house reporter or another more established freelance. The work you put in to creating an exciting, inspiring new angle on a subject has gone to waste – or more accurately to someone else's pay packet – and there's nothing you can do about it. Making sure you get the job means emphasizing the special knowledge you have, the contacts you can talk to or even your unique style of writing.

Once you've generated interest in your work through the pitch you now have to think about the issue of contracts and payment. For many publishers a 'psychological contract' exists between journalist and editor – ie no contract whatsoever. It is up to you to ensure you are guaranteed payment before you start work. When you discuss the piece with the editor you must establish:

1. what precisely the article will be about
2. how long the piece will be (in words)

3. how much money you will receive for this work – and does this include research costs such as phone and travel
4. how you should invoice the publisher and
5. when you can expect to be paid.

It's easy to forget these things when you've just received a commission, and extremely difficult to remedy the situation when you've submitted your work and received no payment.

Establishing yourself as a freelance journalist is not an easy task. If you can get your foot in the door, push it open with all your might. Even after I had been published in the national press I was still scraping a living and constantly pitching to new publishers. Eventually someone suggested my name as a regular contributor for a new section on a newspaper, leading to about three years' continual work. My links with the national press then meant I could think laterally about what I could write about and promote myself to other publishers as an established freelance working on a national daily newspaper. If they didn't believe me I always had my portfolio of cuttings to hand.

One freelance journalist in radio told me he had initially worked for the BBC as part of his work experience during journalism training. From this he was able to build up a great network of contacts and has since worked for a number of different programmes in radio and television.

Freelancing without insanity

There are a couple of ways to enhance your success as a freelance writer and guarantee a reasonable income. First, concentrate on the people you are writing for. When I started out I made sure the copy I submitted was of as high a standard as possible and was always delivered days before the deadline. This built up trust in the editors who used me and encouraged them to pass on my name to other editors in the office. Cultivating a good relationship meant I no longer had to write pitches in order to secure work. I could simply phone up and make a suggestion. Alternatively, a casual conversation aside from work would result in another commission simply because something had just appeared on an editor's desk.

The second method is to become a specialist in what you write about. You don't need to limit yourself to one topic, but generate an area of expertise. My own writing has centred on human resources – but this means I've written about employment law, training issues, public sector management changes and even careers(!). Being involved in the subject on an ongoing basis means I don't have to do loads of research in order to write on a certain topic. I also find I naturally stumble across useful information and stories because people know what I write about.

For some reason there is a kind of glamour to being a freelance writer – maybe it's the idea of being a sole worker, sitting behind a desk in a book-lined study, unleashing wonderful insights into life, the universe and everything. Freelancing does work if you can come up with the goods, negotiate working terms to suit you and turn in good copy. But you also need the self-discipline to sit in a room on your own all day bashing out that copy. There are times when you just can't think of another idea for an article, and when you can't track down the person you need to speak to either to pitch ideas or to get interview material for a commissioned article. There's also an intellectual loneliness – you have to inspire and motivate yourself to find stories and interesting angles.

There are times when you sit looking at a blank computer screen, convinced you will never be able to deliver the copy required. Then there are the times when every pitch you make is rejected and weeks later an article precisely the same as your pitch appears in the magazine you pitched to. There's the head-crunching tedium of research and, of course, the feeling whenever you pick up the phone to talk to an editor that it is you he is rejecting, not your work.

All this is tiring and frustrating. One journalist explained to me that when they went freelance they revelled in their new-found freedom. Ultimately, however, this journalist preferred going back into full-time employment because of the comparative security it gave him. If, after considering all the negative aspects of working alone, you are still enthusiastic about being a freelance, you're already halfway to achieving your goal.

So what of joining a union?

Journalism used to be a closed-shop occupation where entrance was fiercely defended by trade union membership. I've heard some bizarre tales of how carefully each applicant to the National Union of Journalists (NUJ) used to be assessed before being admitted to the union. However, the Conservative government of the 1980s successfully reduced the power of the unions, and this, coupled with the transfer of work on to electronic media has rendered the unions pretty much powerless in the workplace. A few publishers still recognize the NUJ, however, and today membership is picking up again. Branches of the NUJ heartily welcome any newcomer to the industry – even if evidence of publication or competence as a journalist is scant. Students on recognized courses can also gain temporary membership.

Union de-recognition has allowed publishers to employ staff at extremely low rates of pay and there's nothing employees can do about it. In one case the management of a regional newspaper threatened to de-recognize the NUJ unless staff accepted new (and significantly worse) pay and conditions. The new terms were accepted, leaving some wondering what precisely what was the worth of NUJ membership if they couldn't even bargain with the paper.

The most obvious attraction to union membership is securing an international press card. This comes in handy for means of identification when reporting from the scene of events. It will show the police and authorities you are who you say you are and that you should therefore be allowed privileged access to press conferences and other press facilities. However, misuse of the card is frowned upon. A few years ago a card-carrying journalism student was involved in a protest. The student was arrested but claimed to be reporting on the demonstration, not taking part in it. On the one hand the police could have been purposefully ignoring the privileges given to the card holder, but on the other hand the student may have been using the card as protection against prosecution. As a feature writer and interviewer I've used my card only once.

Legal support

The NUJ is doing sterling work to protect the rights of its members and provide legal back-up, particularly when freelances run into problems through late-paying employers. Recently a strong campaign has been waged against the increasing tendency among all publishers to buy 'all rights' from their freelance contributors.

It is worth being aware of the background to 'all rights', as wherever you work you will need to know what your rights are in the material you produce. If a journalist is employed full time, the publisher has all rights to anything that journalist produces. In other words, they can publish the journalist's material in as many different formats and as many times as they want. An article in a newspaper can appear in an anthology, on the publication's website, or on a CD-ROM and the author will receive no extra money at all.

If the article is written by a freelance writer, it is a different story. Freelances sell 'first British rights', that is, the right to publish the article once in the UK. If a publisher wants to use the copy again for other purposes he must pay the author a repeat fee. Naturally publishers would rather not have to pay for subsequent use, and are therefore trying to get journalists to assign all their rights in the work so they have the same status as full-time employees. But while treating their work as if they were full-time employees, the journalists themselves do not receive the benefits of full-time employment – holiday, sickness or pension payments, or even any guarantee of future employment. The campaign to resist 'all rights' purchase has been successful in the main with publishers backing down from their original position. Journalists realize that copyright is an important issue and not something they can simply sign away.

Campaigns have also been led on workplace issues such as repetitive strain injury (RSI) and the safe use of VDUs. RSI can put people out of work permanently – the tiny movements required when using a computer keyboard can lead to aches and pains and even arthritis. Exposure to a VDU screen for too long can damage the eyes. The union is also striving to raise pay levels throughout the industry. It recognizes training standards and provides support to trainees as well as benefits to elderly and cash-starved workers.

The NUJ is actively working for freelance journalists. There is a freelance section and section organizer, focused on their needs, providing useful information about the contracts publishers are trying to foist on journalists, the amount of money you can expect to be paid for the job and general discussions of journalistic news. At the same time, some members of the union can make freelancers feel extremely unwelcome. The animosity felt for workers who are undermining the right of full-time journalists is palpable. In one case I was also asked by a union official whether I was freelance by choice or by necessity. There is a general feeling that no one in their right mind would be a freelance. In spite of everything, this is not actually true.

The value of the union is increasing. Its organization still seems archaic – split into chapels, branches and national representatives – and it can seem an impenetrable mass of bureaucracy to the newcomer. In many ways the NUJ is still trying to move on from the traditional world of journalism and provide services relevant to today's way of working.

The union is wise to the current state of play within the industry, and is constantly pushing to include other areas of journalism – copy writing, layout work and public relations. Perhaps the biggest problem is that nationally the general feeling towards trade unions is not a positive one. Many would-be members expect the union to help them get them work and to provide more benefits. They do not appreciate that the whole point of the union is to bring workers together to help each other. Union membership is particularly useful for freelance journalists. Self-employment can be lonely at the best of times so it is useful to have some kind of regular link to the rest of the workplace – even if it all that amounts to is a magazine and newsletter every month or so.

5

Staying power – and what to do if you haven't got it

Tired of journalism, tired of life. Well, face it: if you don't actually want to continue thinking about what is happening in the outside world, getting involved in what's happening and contributing to the debate, what do you want to do? The urge to get out of journalism shouldn't, by the way, be confused with the blasé attitude which always occurs after you've been in the industry for a while.

The first time you have something published the elation you feel is phenomenal. You feel you've arrived, that the world has taken notice of you and that this is the start of an incredible career. A few more articles under your belt and you've got used to the idea of seeing your name in print. Later on you won't really care if what you've written does get published or not – as long as you get paid. Still later you'll get to the stage where everything you read in the press you'll think is facile and stupid compared to what you could write.

But, seriously, there may come a time when the pressure of deadlines and the frustration of not getting to tell the story you wanted to gets too much and you need to find something else. You may find you just don't want to pick up the phone and start the long run to find the next article. You might hate the idea of talking to a complete stranger, or harassing perfectly innocent people into making a comment about something. If too many people have told you journalists are the scum of the earth, if your name in big bold type no longer inspires you and if you'll throw up next time someone says the word 'advertorial' to you, what can you do next?

Before deserting the word processor, notebook and the tape recorder for good, pause and consider precisely what it is that you dislike about the work you are doing. It may be you dislike the ongoing pressure of deadlines or that you don't like having to get to grips with one story only to immediately move on to another afterwards. There may be other areas of newsroom work more conducive for you.

Other options in the news

Sub-editing is a skilled job which requires knowledge of the subject area of the publication as well as technical skills for using the computer equipment used in laying out pages. While being a journalistic activity it is free from the pressure of chasing stories and interviews. The sub-editor on a technology magazine told me that while some subbing work was extremely dry there was no better way to increase an understanding of the subject.

Ascending to the level of editor – or producer in radio and television news – may also remove the day-to-day grind of journalistic work. You can take a far more strategic overview of the publication, line up all the nice interviews for yourself and get your reporters to do the stressful footwork. Some magazine editing bears little resemblance to the usual image of journalism. I once did a week's work editing two magazines for a small publishing company. It soon became apparent that the magazines existed to sell advertising space. This is true of other publications, but in the case of these magazines the advertising staff had the nice upstairs office with windows and comfy office furniture while I was downstairs in the basement with no windows, on the same desk as the page co-ordinator (spending all day laying out advertisements) and the debt collector (spending all day on the phone yelling at late payers). There was no mention of making contacts within those areas in the industry covered by the magazines, no mention of interviews or commissioning articles. The job was really just a copy-writing one – take information from one source and rewrite it to fill the magazine.

The work was clearly less hectic and high pressured. But there was very little space for creativity in pushing the editorial content of the magazine. I didn't stay there because I needed more of a challenge.

Production management – pulling together the text and pictures for the publication and assembling them ready for the printers – is another area of journalistic work which does not require going out and getting the material. It can be a more creative, artistic pursuit – but production managers still get very, very stressed as printing day approaches and not all the material has arrived.

The great thing about being a journalist is that you could simply transfer your print-related skills into broadcast-related skills or vice versa. Once you've established yourself as a good journalist you don't need to get stuck in a rut with the same publication or subject matter. You can gain new skills or offer your exceptional talents to a new medium. Indeed, one journalist, trained extensively in the printed media, told me he believed newspapers were on the way out. Digital television, the Internet and broadcast media would be where people went for their news and, therefore, he retrained to get into this area.

More words, please

Market research companies may prove a lucrative market for your skills. Having produced a whole load of data they require someone to take a view of the information, interpret the results and form an overview of the research. Many companies are keen to use journalists in this area because they are more likely to find a coherent story – one that will be picked up by editors and readers – than a research analyst. Many journalists suddenly find themselves writing books. They may be factual, relating to what they have been reporting on for a living or they may start writing creatively – a complete contrast to the nature of their previous work. Alternatively, they may write about the lifestyles they have seen and studied over their years as journalists.

A US commentator believes book writing is one of the few ways in which journalists can secure a guaranteed income of over $30,000. The argument is that the book advance – the money paid to the author before the book has been produced – negates the necessity to write several articles over that period of time. If the book is well promoted and successful, further payments from royalties, translation and even broadcast rights will still arrive in the future. A book gives journalists more space to expand upon a subject, to indulge themselves rather than keeping strictly to the style of their journalism work. In practice, it's not quite so clear cut. Yes, it is nice to write something longer for a change, but some journalists can find the prospect of hundreds of blank pages a complete non-starter. In spite of the longer deadline you may still find yourself bashing text out at midnight before the day of your submission. Yes, you do get an advance, but without careful negotiation this may not mean you can drop everything else you're doing and concentrate on your masterpiece. And while the idea of being paid an advance is attractive the payment could more accurately be called a 'late'.

Book publishing, just like journalism, is a question of fashion. Some publications have proven to be runaway successes as they tap into the *Zeitgeist* of the time. Some authors have been able to build up a reputation before they've even committed one word to paper, resulting in agent interest and the ability to negotiate brilliant deals.

If your journalism work means you know what the current market place is interested in you can identify precisely the subjects and styles which will sell. And having been sent thousands of press releases from people wanting you to mention their products, services and mere existence in your journalism you should also have a shrewd idea of how to put together an effective marketing campaign for your own work.

Tell me about it

Alternatively, these kinds of skills will win you favour in an independent PR company. Once again, the insight a journalist has into the creation of the news is a valuable marketing tool for an agency. Journalists may have direct contacts in the press of use to the agency, but more likely they will be able to spot angles and contemporary stories that can be used to promote a client. Journalists will know precisely the kind of information a newsroom needs and may be able to provide interview training for PR clients. As someone on the receiving end of press releases, faxes and emails over a number of years, I know how often I want to hear from a PR company and when it becomes overkill. PR and marketing work can also mean co-ordinating conferences and booking guest speakers. Your knowledge of the industry will mean you can create a well-balanced line-up of speakers and cover all the main topics which need debate.

At one extreme, you may find your frustration with the world of journalism such that you want to publish your own magazine or newspaper in order to put across what you think people should be reading about. And doing that is now a fairly simple process. Of course you need loads of financial backing to set up the operation and you'll have to be sure what you are about to publish is going to sell – or at least will sell advertising space – or your financial backers will not be too pleased. At the other extreme you may be sick and tired of staring at a word processor and want to get out of the system altogether.

In the current climate, tarnished spirits and less than 100 per cent given to the job is likely to result in you being ousted before you've even noticed you don't want to work there any more. There are probably far more ex-journalists wondering how they can get back into the industry than there are trying to pursue a different career.

Some journalists, having spent their working lives in journalism, find they're able to pass on their experience and skills through the education system. This may range from simply providing advice to would-be journalists, through to teaching full courses on the skills and methods of journalism. To some extent education is still using the principal skills of the journalist – collecting and communicating information in a positive and understandable manner.

Watching from the sidelines

One former journalist I know claimed to have left the industry because he 'couldn't stand the ethics'. The comment was meant light-heartedly to some degree but I got the feeling what he disliked was the way in which the press tends to generalize and gloss over the details when presenting stories, rather than allowing time and space for the real issues to be discussed. Attention-grabbing tabloid head-lines are one example of this but it still happens in the trade press. There is always the pressure to find cutting-edge, life-changing stories and to present these in a way no reader can overlook. It may not mean distorting the facts in order to get the story, but a matter of emphasizing some elements above others.

This particular ex-journo started up his own communications company. This was not simply a PR agency but a consultancy which would get involved with the activities of their clients, identifying the reasons for any bad press they received and then seeking to do something about that coverage by altering the way the company did business. The change of process would then be promoted to the press rather than simply giving a new image and hoping people would forget the past.

This career change was not particularly remarkable. An engineer by training, he had spent a few years in the industry before getting involved with the publishing side. At first, his expertise was valued and he worked across many publications, rising from reporter through to the section editor of a national daily. Having achieved this post he realized he was feeling frustrated because he wasn't actually doing anything 'hands-on'. Sure he was able to uncover stories, identify problems and pinpoint issues which needed addressing but, at the end of the day, real change depended on the readership acting on the information he gave in his articles.

He discussed his feelings with a colleague who worked for a major engineering group. Partly kidding and partly challenging the apparent arrogance of the know-it-all journalist in front of him, this colleague challenged him to pitch a proposal to remedy an issue within his own company. The journalist took the opportunity with both hands and from that his work took a completely different direction. Twelve months later he'd set up his own company and was playing a part within the industry he'd previously viewed from the outside only.

This particular example shows how someone moved in and out of journalism – using their knowledge and expertise to gain a writing position – before moving back into the practical side of things again as they found they wanted to change their involvement. Some say today's business world is made up of consultants – and it is true there are niche markets for people with good advice and skills in many areas of work. Your involvement as a journalist can easily bring to light opportunities for future career moves. In a completely different industry it's worth noting that Neil Tennant was originally a writer for the pop magazine *Smash Hits* before founding the Pet Shop Boys and having a successful musical career.

A new scene

If you are searching for a new workplace, a change of scenery in which to practise journalism, many large companies employ writers to take care of their in-house publications. There may be staff magazines to edit and write, newsletters to compile and even official documents to proof read and re-write. In such a context you may find yourself responsible for all areas of producing material – but this may also be the kind of challenge you want – to be able to control the style of your publication as well as content. There may be ghost-writing work on behalf of various people in the organization – the company director may think he knows what he wants to say but be unable to put it into words. A trained journalist, used to working sensitively with words and interviewees, will be able to write or rewrite the director's ideas in a clear and concise manner.

Many companies are now investing in Internet sites for company use internally and externally. These, too, require good writers – computer-literate yes – but principally able to ensure the material on the site is well presented and managed. Just because there appears to be unlimited space on the Web for publishing information doesn't mean absolutely everything should wind up being held electronically.

Technology offers many opportunities for journalists and creative writers. It is not simply creating the text which appears on World Wide Web sites, but multimedia technology requires good writing and editing skills. You may not understand how the technology works but it's another media for your work. Writers are constantly sought by the CD-ROM industry – not simply for collating and editing material for publication, but even in the creation of interactive games – audio-visual games where the player follows a story line and carefully worked out plot in order to achieve the object of the game.

The fast pace of change in technology means the future of the industry cannot be predicted. There has been speculation on how electronic books and newspapers will put press and broadcast news services out of business, but this is unlikely. A background in journalism means you are unlikely to be without some role in the information-rich society of the future. No matter what the media turns out to be, it will always require people who can collect, sift, interpret and present information to a waiting public.

Appendix:
For what it's worth

The NUJ are currently campaigning to ensure all journalists are paid at least £10,000 per year. Sadly they cannot enforce this and there are many cases where this level is simply not met. Trainees in their first position can earn as little as £6,000pa. With many first-time journalists having already taken out loans in order to pay for training and qualifications it can be nearly impossible to survive at this level of remuneration. There are new journalists working now whose annual pay is not as much as their debts.

Another example of pitiful remuneration came from a local newspaper which was trying to recruit a fully trained news reporter with their own car. The amount of money offered was actually less than it would have cost to hire a car on a daily basis – thus the newspaper was not really offering enough money to cover the running costs of the vehicle.

Only around 20 per cent of journalists earn £35,000 or more. Most journalists earn somewhere between £15,000 and £20,000, depending on their experience and their market worth. Staff writers on newspapers and magazines can expect to earn roughly £12,000 to £15,000 as a starting salary and production editors £16,000 upwards. Apple Mac operators – page designers and sub-editors – can get between £16,000 and £20,000. Broadcast rates for radio and television are generally higher, in some cases as much as £10,000 more. Two to three years' experience will increase your income, perhaps by as much as £3,000 – not very substantial. A managing editor or features editor can earn around £18,000 to £20,000, but it is only when you reach the national papers and magazines that you can be assured of a salary above £20,000 or so.

One staff writer commented that editorial work within a publishing house was generally badly paid. Having established his salary, the publisher seemed almost obliged to get every drop of energy out of him before hinting at increasing the pay packet. In this case, the only way to hike up his income was to take freelance work in addition to his usual obligations.

In general, freelance writing pays by the word. Some people find this a strange way to charge – finding the idea of not being paid by the day a little odd – but there are benefits all round. Clearly the publisher pays the freelance according to the amount of space covered by the article. At the same time the freelance knows exactly how much he is to be paid regardless of how much time it will take him to do the work. This means you can get paid the same amount of money for a piece which takes you half a day to research and write, as for one which takes you three days. Since research is likely to be spread out over a number of days, it can be difficult to say exactly how much time is taken by each article you write.

The rate charge per word depends on the type of publication. The minimum rate should be around £130 per 1,000 words going up to as much as £350. The rise in rates corresponds to the amount of money charged for advertising in each publication. Clearly, the more upmarket and popular the publication, the greater the advertising revenue and the greater the fee to the journalist. It's up to the individual freelance to bargain for the highest rate possible. There may be factors which you can use to hike up the fee: a short deadline for you to deliver the article, your own expertise on the subject or access to a completely exclusive story every other paper will want to get.

Many publishers pay freelance writers when their article is published rather than upon submission of the text. This seems completely unfair since the journalist has already carried out the research and the writing work, and incurred costs to do so. Things get worse: once the article is published you may still find you have to wait a month or even longer before you get that cheque. Freelance writers can soon find themselves subsidizing the production of magazines by large publishing houses.

Some publishers claim that they understand the difficulties this situation can cause for freelances – who are generally one-man/ woman bands and can ill afford to wait while an accounts department pulls itself together for the next cheque run. Some have agreed to pay on acceptance of text (which means at least 21 days after the acceptance of text), but don't hold your breath: there are bound to be other bits of bureaucracy which delay your payment.

Freelances working on shifts for newspapers and news broadcasters may be able to bargain for improved rates, but in general BBC local radio will pay just over £80.00 per day, while regional reporters on national programmes should earn over £100.00 per day. Interviews and feature programmes for radio are paid for by each minute of broadcast time and as a rough outline you might get around £170.00 for a seven-minute piece.

The NUJ's freelance guide now even carries basic rates for Internet work. These include £150.00 per page set up on the World Wide Web and up to £50.00 an hour or £350.00 a day to manage website production.

Other areas of journalistic work – PR, copywriting and so on – present a similar picture. The higher salaries can be demanded by those who have established a strong reputation in their field. Media relations managers will start off their careers at £12,000 or less, depending on the organization or company they are working for. This can rise to between £30,000 and £40,000 after five or six years of hard slog and tactical self-marketing. High salaries are there for the taking, however. For example, a national newspaper editor will be able to demand a salary of £80,000 upwards. There are also some celebrity/notorious columnists who are able to charge hundreds of thousands of pounds for what they do – even when what they produce is only a few hundred words of opinion each week. The opportunities are there for the taking – it's up to you to aim high, work hard and give your readers exactly what they want.